Healing Prayer:
Spiritual Pathways to Health and Wellness

Healing Prayer:
Spiritual Pathways to Health and Wellness

BARBARA SHLEMON RYAN

SERVANT
BOOKS

PUBLISHED BY ST. ANTHONY MESSENGER PRESS
CINCINNATI, OHIO

ISBN 1-56955-262-2

Copyright © 2001 by Barbara Shlemon Ryan. All rights reserved.

Published by Servant Books, an imprint of St. Anthony Messenger Press
28 W. Liberty St.
Cincinnati, OH 45202
www. AmericanCatholic.org

Printed in the United States of America
Printed on acid-free paper

05 06 07 08 09 10 9 8 7 6 5 4 3 2

CONTENTS

FOREWORD

Back in 1969 I first met Barbara when she came up and introduced herself at a retreat I was giving in Racine, Wisconsin. She was a little desperate, because she was a faithful Roman Catholic who had learned about praying for healing at a time no other Catholics she knew about were doing it. She was delighted to find someone else in her Church who had made the same discovery: that an ordinary Christian could pray for the sick and they might actually be healed. It didn't take me long to realize that here was a woman with a remarkable healing gift, and we quickly welcomed her to our team. We had come from St. Louis, Missouri. As a result she spent that weekend praying for dozens of people for inner healing, most of then nuns. Since she first began praying for the sick back in 1964, she was perhaps the very first Roman Catholic layperson to become involved in a full-time healing ministry.

Barbara has not only persevered over these years but has become widely recognized, not only as gifted in praying, but also as an excellent speaker and author. I have seen God use her in remarkable healing sessions. I recall one time in India, for example, when she was on the platform and, pointing off to her right, said, "There is

someone over here who has a broken right femur, and
God is healing him."

And it was true.

But her greatest gift has really been her ability to
encourage thousands of ordinary people to pray for the
sick, and them to teach them in down-to-earth ways how
to do it. She has given thousands of talks and has spoken
effectively in such far countries as Bolivia, India, Costa
Rica, Venezuela, and Ireland.

Some speakers who are gifted with dramatic healing
gifts can come across as a little extreme, but Barbara's
approach has always been true to life and yet very powerful and moving. Jesus has gifted her particularly in
praying for inner healing ("healing of the memories"),
and, following Agnes Sanford, she was a pioneer in teaching about this important area of healing.

In 1975 she was instrumental in founding the
Association of Christian Therapists, an organization dedicated to encouraging those in the healing professions—
such as physicians, counselors and nurses—to pray for
healing. In the early days Barbara was a courageous
pioneer in bringing healing to her Church and to her
profession (she was a psychiatric nurse) in spite of their
skepticism and even opposition. Now that she is in
demand as a speaker from those same groups—churches

and medical groups—she accepts the praise that comes her way with grace.

If you are looking for a brief book, presenting the essentials of healing prayer in a simple, balanced, effective way, with plenty of interesting stories to illustrate the main points, look no further. This is your book!

Francis S. MacNutt, Ph.D.
President, Christian Healing Ministries

INTRODUCTION

One night in 1964, the Lord taught me a lesson about his love that would change my understanding of suffering and, ultimately, the course of my life.

As a registered nurse, I was employed in a small community hospital in northern Illinois, assigned to a medical-surgical ward. I worked the 3 P.M. to 11 P.M. shift and had received a report from the day nurses indicating one patient in a comatose condition would probably expire during the night. Her diagnosis, cirrhosis of the liver, and the circumstances of her life were particularly sad. The patient was a young mother of three small children; she had put up a valiant fight for life during her stay in the hospital.

As I entered her room to check the flow of her intravenous bottles, I was overcome with sorrow. The woman's weight had dropped to ninety pounds, most of it concentrated in fluid in her abdomen, giving the appearance of a nine-month pregnancy. Her arms and legs were like toothpicks, she had lost all the hair on her body, and jaundice colored her skin a deep orange-yellow. She did not appear to respond to stimuli of any kind; her breathing was shallow and irregular.

I glanced at her distraught husband sitting across the room and wished there were words to convey some comfort to his heart. The death of his wife seemed very near.

Back at the nurse's station, I confessed my feelings of inadequacy to Harriet, the other nurse on duty with me. She agreed that the situation was grave but didn't believe it was hopeless. I knew Harriet to be a devout Episcopalian with deep faith that God really answers prayer. I felt, however, she was being unrealistic in believing God could or would intervene in this case. As a Roman Catholic, I believed miracles happened at shrines like Lourdes and Fatima, but I didn't expect such happenings to occur in ordinary places.

Undaunted by my skepticism, Harriet approached the husband with the suggestion that he contact his parish priest to anoint his wife with the Sacrament of Extreme Unction. For many years this sacrament of anointing with oil was looked upon as a preparation for death, the final unction. She explained that the recent Vatican Council had restored the concept of this sacrament to its original emphasis, the Sacrament of the Sick. It was to be administered as a means of healing.*

The husband took a long while to consider this action and finally decided there was no other recourse. The priest who answered the phone arrived at the hospital within minutes. He quietly read through the ritual, pausing at intervals to apply oil to the sick woman's body. He also brought the Holy Eucharist with him in the form of a small host, but the woman was too comatose to receive Communion. The priest gently touched her lips with the Body of Christ and left the hospital.

The entire procedure had taken only a few minutes, and there were no observable changes in the patient's condition. I went off duty feeling very depressed and believing we had instilled hope in a hopeless situation.

I was back on duty the next afternoon. As I walked past the dying woman's room, I glanced in and froze in my tracks. She was sitting up at the side of the bed sipping soup and talking to her husband and some of the nurs-

---

*The new Rite of Anointing encourages the whole church to recognize healing prayer as a normal factor in our Christian lives. Family, friends, and caregivers are invited to join the priest in praying for the sick person. The letter to James gives the scriptural directive, "If one of you is ill, he should send for the elders of the church, and they must anoint him with oil in the name of the Lord and pray over him. The prayer of faith will save the sick man and the Lord will raise him up again; and if he has committed any sins, he will be forgiven. So confess your sins to one another, and pray for one another, and this will cure you" (James 5:13-16).

ing staff. The day nurse walked by me and said, matter-of-factly, "She took a turn for the better last night."

Her health continued to improve as laboratory reports demonstrated a completely functioning liver. Within three weeks she was released from the hospital and restored to her grateful family.

Other hospital personnel met my excitement over this event with pessimism and unbelief. Most of the doctors and nurses called it a "spontaneous remission" and expected she would soon experience a relapse (she never did). Only one physician admitted the possibility of divine intervention. He was a Jewish doctor who had been a part of her medical team. After reviewing all the data he said, "We didn't do this; God did."

* * *

My initiation into the healing power of Jesus Christ had begun and I could hardly contain my curiosity on the subject. Harriet invited me to attend prayer meetings at Holy Trinity Episcopal Church in Wheaton, Illinois. (Such meetings were nonexistent in my denomination at that time.)

I was greatly impressed with the faith of the participants and their ability to talk confidently to God from their hearts. They seemed really to believe God was listening. I longed for such an intimate relationship with the Lord. Fr. Richard Winkler, the Episcopal priest who was leading the sessions, must have sensed my desire because he asked if I wanted to receive the gifts of the Holy Spirit in my life.

I didn't fully understand the question but I was willing to accept anything the Father wanted to give me. He invited the prayer group to join him as he gently laid his hands on my head and asked the Holy Spirit to activate all the gifts given when I received the Sacrament of Confirmation. A surge of joy entered my heart as I began to "speak in tongues." I had never experienced such a sense of God's loving presence. I remember staying awake the entire night, afraid if I went to sleep the awesome presence of the Holy Spirit would disappear.

The loving members of the prayer group encouraged me to remain faithful in attending the Catholic Church and to join their meetings whenever possible. Frequently they would join me in praying for spiritual renewal throughout the Christian churches. Two years later, in 1967, when new stirrings of the Holy Spirit began at Catholic universities such as Notre Dame and Duquesne, I understood the wisdom of their discernment.

My education regarding the effectiveness of Christian

healing prayer was greatly enhanced through the books and teachings of Agnes Sanford. She and her husband, Edgar, an Episcopal priest, established a School of Pastoral Care to teach clergy and healthcare professionals how to pray for the sick. Attending four of these schools gave me the confidence to believe that I could be an instrument of God's power.

In addition, Fr. Winkler introduced me to the International Order of St. Luke the Physician (OSL).* Formed in 1932, the International Order of St. Luke the Physician is an organization dedicated to promoting the restoration of healing as taught and demonstrated by Jesus Christ. Using their guidelines, I began reading the Scriptures and discovered the great number of Gospel texts that deal with healing.

I had grown up with a belief that God sent sickness and suffering to promote spiritual growth. One of the books I was advised to read was *A Reporter Finds God Through*

---

*Its membership is made up of medical professionals, clergy of all Christian denomications and laity. For further information contact: OSL., P.O. Box 13701, San Antonio, Texas, 78213.

**Emily was a professional writer who began her career as a journalist during World War II. Her original intention was to debunk the ministry of healing, so she set out to uncover charlatans in action. She carefully recorded her conversations with believers and unbelievers as she painstakingly pursued every line of controversy surrounding healing prayer. The end result was her own conversion and subsequent ordination as a deaconess in the Episcopal church.

Spiritual Healing by Emily Gardner Neal.** Her words convinced me to continue in my quest for understanding. "If you sincerely feel that God wills sickness," she said, "then you must reject all medical treatment because you are deliberately working against God's will as you conceive it to be."

This simple statement proved a turning point for my spiritual and professional life. I began to recognize the role of healthcare professionals as an extension of the Father's healing love. It seemed obvious to me that it was God who blessed the competence of a surgeon, the wisdom of a diagnostician, the benefits of medications, the value of therapies and the proficiency of nurses. However, in the sixties and seventies, it was not uncommon for the medical community to equate Christian healing with "tent revivals" and the narrow-minded methods of zealous evangelists admonishing people to "claim their healing" and "throw away their medicine."

It's interesting to compare such a pessimistic outlook with today's convergence of faith and medicine. More than thirty medical schools in the United States, including Mayo Medical School, teach courses in spirituality and healing. That's up from just three schools in 1995.

There is an enormous body of evidence (over one hundred experiments, many conducted under stringent conditions) showing that prayer brings about significant changes in a variety of living beings. These experiments have prompted many healthcare professionals to ask themselves, "Are you going to follow these scientific directions and actually use prayer?" Many are now trying, with dramatic results.

From the beginning of my spiritual journey I was convinced that healing prayer was an integral component of my nursing profession. Each time I prayed with patients they reported feelings of peace and serenity. Even if the medical diagnosis remained critical, their faith level seemed to increase. However, this newfound dimension of caregiving caused me to question God's plan for my life. I spent many agonizing months trying to sort out the conflict between my deep desire to care for the sick and my equally strong yearning to concentrate on the spiritual dimension of wellness. My quest was finally resolved one night in 1965.

I had worked nearly an hour of overtime in order to complete the charting that had been neglected while I busied myself praying with patients. After midnight, as I drove into the driveway of our home and turned off the ignition, the presence of the Lord seemed to fill the car. His closeness triggered a torrent of tears as I poured out my frustrations and confusions concerning my vocation.

Deep within my heart I felt Jesus asking if I was willing to put away my cap and uniform and follow him. My whole being resisted the invitation with numerous arguments. There is such a shortage of nurses. What about the time, energy, and money that went into my education?

The voice within persistently requested an answer. Was I willing to put my chosen career on the "altar" and embark on a new journey? It seemed as if I sat in the car for hours while the battle raged within me. Finally, I tearfully abandoned myself to the Lord, agreed to resign my hospital position, and was flooded with an overwhelming sense of peace. No lightning bolts flashed through the sky; I just knew that I had done the right thing.

It was three years from the time of that decision until I discovered God directing me to teach others to pray for the sick. In my wildest imaginings, I would never have considered such a ministry and still feel woefully inadequate for the task. Surrendering my will to God has given me ample opportunity to discover the awesomeness of walking in the footsteps of Jesus.

For eleven years I was privileged to teach in Latin America, Europe, and Asia as part of a team ministry headed by Francis MacNutt. In 1988, I founded Beloved Ministry, an evangelistic organization dedicated to preaching, teaching, and healing. Along with my husband, Tim, we endeavor to bring the message of healing to all who seek wellness.

Often I receive encouraging letters that confirm once more the importance of the "yes" I said so many years ago. From Canada: "Your recent healing service brought much relief from the physical pain associated with the auto accident I had seven years ago. I've been able to return to work and have joined a prayer group in my church. I want to help others discover the power of healing in their lives."

What about those who retain their infirmities despite repeated prayer efforts? Years of experience have taught me to stop expending energy asking, "Why aren't they all healed?" and to recognize the problem is too complex for my mind. I've learned to direct my efforts toward praying for the sick, leaving the results up to the Creator who is all-knowing and all-loving. I have absolutely no doubts that God wants wholeness for all of us and awaits the day when "there will be ... no more death, and no more mourning or sadness. The world of the past has gone" (Rv 21:4).

Until that day, I believe we have the responsibility to keep the light of Jesus Christ burning on the earth. Our prayers can do much to hasten his return.

Chapter One

Who Has the Gift of Healing?

These are the signs that will be associated with believers: in my name, they ... will lay their hands on the sick, who will recover.

MARK 16:17

Jesus performed many works of healing as he walked upon the earth. Whenever he encountered people who were suffering, he alleviated their pain and restored them to wholeness.

Most Christians don't have difficulty believing that the Lord possessed the gifts of healing necessary to mend a sick body. We read the scriptural accounts of healing and we wish Jesus were here to cure the sick of today's world. Medicine and technology have made great strides in recent years, yet many conditions remain incurable. An aging population presents new problems that are seemingly insurmountable. The charism of healing would be greatly prized.

The good news is, we do have the healing love of Jesus Christ with us today. The gifts of healing as manifested by the Lord have been delegated to each person who accepts Jesus as Savior.

Before he was crucified, Jesus said to his disciples, "Whoever believes in me will perform the same works as I do myself, he will perform even greater works, because I am going to the Father" (Jn 14:12). Jesus was telling the disciples that ministering to the blind and the lame was not going to stop when he was no longer visible. The commission to carry on the healing work was given to "whoever believes" in him. The works would be even greater because they were no longer performed by only one person, but by everyone who professes Jesus as Lord.

Jesus invited us to be extensions of himself so that multitudes of people could be touched and cured by his love. He has no hands to lay on the sick but our hands. If, as Christians, we really believe the Lord dwells within us, then it should not come as a surprise that we can pray for the sick and they will be healed. We merely provide the instrument through which the love of God can shine forth.

Christians are accustomed to thinking that the gift of healing is reserved for certain individuals who receive a supernatural "call" from God. We read the lives of the saints and find it difficult or impossible to emulate their heroic acts of holiness and piety. Therefore, we conclude that we couldn't possibly imitate their works of healing. We hear the word "miracles" and think of the shrines at Lourdes and Fatima; seldom do we consider that Jesus expects *us* to do such works. If it is true that God "does not have favorites" (Acts 10:34), then each of us is invited to develop his or her relationship with God to its fullest potential.

One typical excuse for not exercising the gift of healing is "I'm not worthy." It is a common human trait to feel inadequate in the realm of holiness; most people believe they have a long way to go before God could use them. Most withdraw from commitment in a futile effort to attain some level of perfection.

It is true that God expects us to remove sinful behavior from our lives and to live in harmony with those around us. The good news is that Jesus Christ came to save us, "while we were still sinners" (Rom 5:8), and he wants to use us with all our weaknesses and inadequacies. Most of the people elevated to sainthood seemed to be painfully aware of their "unworthiness," yet they allowed the light of God to shine through them to others. As long as we are aware of our faults, doing what we can to correct them, then we can completely rely on God's goodness, strength, and holiness.

The following story clearly illustrates our role.

A man was sleeping in his cabin one night when suddenly his room filled with light, and the Savior appeared. The Lord told the man he had work for him to do, and showed him a large rock in front of his cabin. The Lord explained that the man was to push against the rock with all his might. So, this the man did; day after day. For many years he toiled from sunup to sundown; his shoulders set squarely against the cold, massive surface of the unmoving rock, pushing with all his might. Each night the man returned to his cabin sore and worn out, feeling that his whole day had been spent in vain.

Since the man was showing signs of discouragement, the devil decided to enter the picture by placing thoughts into the man's weary mind: *You have been pushing against that rock for a long time, and it hasn't budged. Why kill yourself over this? You are never going to move it.* Thus, the evil one gave the man the impression that the task was impossible. These thoughts discouraged and disheartened the man, and made him feel like a failure. *Why kill myself over this?"* he thought. *"I'll put in my time, giving just the minimum effort. That will be good enough.*

So that is what he planned to do, until one day he

decided to make it a matter of prayer and take his troubled thoughts to the Lord. "Lord," he said, "I have labored long and hard in your service, putting all my strength into doing what you have asked. Yet, after all this time, I have not even budged that rock by half a millimeter. What is wrong? Why am I failing?"

The Lord responded compassionately, "My friend, when I asked you to serve me and you accepted, I told you that your task was to push against the rock with all your strength, which you have done. Never once did I mention to you that I expected you to move it. Your task was to push. Now you come to me with your strength spent, thinking that you have failed. But, is that really so?

"Look at yourself. Your arms are strong and muscled, your back sinewy and brown, your hands are callused from constant pressure, and your legs have become massive and hard. Through opposition you have grown much, and your abilities now surpass that which you used to have. You haven't moved the rock, but your calling was to be obedient and to push and to exercise your faith and trust in my wisdom. This you have done. Now I, my friend, will move the rock."

Author Unknown

Those who are most effective in the healing ministry have accepted their own limitations by exercising simple obedience and faith in God's power to move mountains. We're of little value to God when we are self-reliant and dependent upon our own strength. One woman told me she believed God was asking her to pray for others but she consistently refused, saying, "I'm not ready yet." Her hesitancy melted away after hearing the Lord say, "When you're ready, I won't need you." It's not our *ability* but our *availability* that can make us useful instruments for God's purposes.

After I witnessed the young woman's healing from cirrhosis of the liver, I began to experiment with prayer. I reasoned that, if a sacrament could produce such dramatic results, perhaps my simple prayers might be sufficient to comfort some of my patients. Therefore, I decided to look for opportunities to pray with the sick who were in my care. I had no previous training in prayer techniques, but I did have a deep desire to relieve suffering and see people healed. I was willing to be a fool for Christ if it could help someone.

My first opportunity was an elderly man in the advanced stages of cancer. He was in great pain, requiring heavy doses of narcotics, constantly retching and vomiting. One afternoon, as I was administering his injection, I asked if he would like me to say a prayer with him. He clutched my hand very tightly and said, "Would you please ask God to help me?" I said a brief word about God loving him enough to die for him and we recited the Lord's Prayer together. The old gentleman fell into a quiet, restful sleep and I left the room. He lived for several more weeks before he died, but needed no more pain medication and had no other episodes of vomiting. Could it have been a coincidence or the power of suggestion at work in this situation? The explanation seems secondary to the fact that a human being was relieved of misery. I decided to continue experimenting.

A few days later, we admitted an eighty-three-year-old man who was scheduled for prostate surgery. His surgeon was concerned that the operation might be too great a strain for the man's weakened heart, but the enlarged prostate had to be removed. The night before the operation, I went into the patient's room to prepare him for sleep. I asked if he would like to pray for a restful night and he readily agreed. After a short prayer, he seemed more relaxed and less anxious about his surgery. The next morning, the hospital orderly transported him to the operating room at 8:00 and returned him to the room at 8:30. No surgery was performed because the prostate was no longer enlarged.

These answered prayers captured the attention of one of the licensed practical nurses assigned to work with Harriet and me. (Harriet is the nurse I mentioned in the introduction of this book.) She conceived the idea of gathering together an intercessory prayer group composed of hospital personnel, who would pray for the needs of the staff and the patients.

On our 3 P.M. to 11 P.M. shift, the only available time for such a meeting was during the evening coffee break. Since the hospital had no chapel, six people began to gather for prayer each evening in the operating room. Few outside of the group knew about the meeting, but the entire facility seemed to benefit from those quiet moments of intercessory prayer.

During that time we would often pray for our more critical patients and their families. Sometimes these prayers brought definite changes in patients' physical conditions; sometimes it gave them courage and confidence in facing surgical procedures; sometimes it provided consolation to dying patients. Always prayer seemed to be a positive influence, bringing peace to anxious hearts.

Perhaps these outcomes were "coincidences," but we came to discover that coincidences seemed to happen more readily when prayer was applied. These experiences convinced me that praying for others is an essential component of Christianity and all believers are to "do the works" that Jesus did.

Prayer for Healers

Lord make me an instrument of your health:
where there is sickness, let me bring cure;
where there is injury, aid;
where there is suffering, ease;
where there is sadness, comfort;
where there is despair, hope;
where there is death, acceptance and peace.

Grant that I may not so much seek to
be justified, as to console;
to be obeyed, as to understand;
to be honored, as to love;
for it is in giving ourselves that we heal,
it is in listening that we comfort,
and it is in dying that we are born to
ETERNAL LIFE.

Modified from the prayer
attributed to St. Francis

uidance

Whatever you ask for in my name I will do, so that the Father may be glorified in the Son. If you ask for anything in my name, I will do it.

JOHN 14:14

"If God is all-knowing then he knows my needs and I don't have to ask him for anything." This rationale is used by many who think prayer is a lazy approach to life's problems. "God helps those who help themselves," they say, oblivious to the fact that Jesus came to help those who couldn't help themselves. This doesn't imply that we sit back and passively wait for the Lord to handle every detail, but it does teach us to allow Jesus to become a partner in working out the answers to our prayers.

Jesus taught his disciples, "Your Father knows what you need before you ask him" (Mt 6:8), then he went on to teach them the Lord's Prayer so they would know how to ask. Our relationship was not to be a passive

dependence on the Father's love but an actively coop-
erative effort in obtaining our "daily bread." The Lord
provides for many of our needs without our petitioning
for his help. Yet he also tells us "Ask and you will receive,
and so your joy will be complete" (Jn 16:24).

We have been given free will; therefore, the Lord does
not take us for granted nor violate the sanctity of our
individuality. When the two blind men shouted to Jesus,
"Lord! have pity on us, Son of David," he asked them,
"What do you want me to do for you?" He didn't auto-
matically assume they wanted to be healed of their sight-
lessness. Only after they requested, "Lord, let us have our
sight back," did he touch their eyes and restore them
(see Mt 20:29-34).

How many desires of our hearts go unanswered
because we fail to ask? We also fail to take into account
the second part of the Lord's teaching, which admon-
ishes us to ask in his name (see Jn 16:23). This doesn't
mean tacking the name of Jesus Christ to the end of all
our prayers like some magic formula for success. Jesus
was addressing himself to Jews who understood that a
person's name signified his destiny, personality, and
character. Jewish parents took great care in naming their
children because the name would indicate the direction
and meaning of their lives.

There are scriptural examples of individuals' names being changed after they were called into a deeper commitment to God's purposes. For example, Sarah, Abraham, Peter, and Paul were renamed to reflect their new persona. When Jesus instructs us to ask in his name "he is teaching us to pray in his personality and character. He wants us to develop the same kind of intimate relationship he had with the Father so our prayers will always be answered.

This kind of relationship cannot be achieved overnight but requires us to continually immerse ourselves in the presence of Jesus until we become conformed to his image and likeness. Daily scripture reading (particularly from the Gospels), along with time for private and community prayer and time for meditating on devotional writings, can aid in realizing this goal.

We often fail to ask for God's help because we believe our needs are too trivial for his consideration. This limits the Lord's involvement in our lives since we pray only during crisis situations. If we don't see God answering prayer in little things, it will be difficult to trust him when disasters come upon us. Faith builds with experience and can be strengthened through consistent exercise.

Jesus also taught that our prayers would be answered so the Father would be glorified in the Son (see Jn 14:13).

This can only occur if we are seeking to do the Father's will through our intercessions. Many times our prayer requests don't bear fruit because we have neglected to discover what the Lord wanted in the situation. We assume that his will is the same as ours without first asking for his guidance.

For many years I prayed for the conversion of my first husband. It never entered my thoughts that our Lord might have something else in mind. When nothing seemed to be happening, I finally realized that I had not consulted God, and so instead I prayed for guidance. The Holy Spirit revealed that I was praying for the wrong person to be changed; I was the one who needed transforming. There were many areas in my own life where I was not being submissive, forgiving, and loving. Turning the spotlight onto my own spiritual growth was a definite step in bringing greater harmony into our household.

Seeking the Lord's guidance is an essential factor in healing prayer. It's important to spend time listening to the instructions of the Holy Spirit so our prayers can become more effective. We begin by asking, "Lord, what do you want in this situation?" and then pray in accordance with his leading. It takes practice to develop this kind of "listening heart," but the more we test these inner messages and prove their accuracy, the more we will be able to rely on them. We might ask for the "gift of ears" as well as the gift of tongues.

Our prayer group was once asked to pray for a young boy who was dying of kidney failure. We joined together and asked God to touch his body and restore him to health. Several prophecies were given indicating that he was being healed, but the hospital report showed further deterioration in his condition. We again gathered for prayer, but this time asked the guidance of the Holy Spirit. One of the women in the group received an inner feeling that the boy's mother was an obstacle to the flow of God's power. She discerned the mother's fears were so great that they were creating a spiritual barrier between him and the Lord. She suggested we pray for the mother rather than the son.

We interceded in this manner, asking God to give the mother an overwhelming sense of his presence so she could believe his love was greater than hers could ever be. She later reported to us that she received a powerful anointing of love as she sat at her son's bedside. She knew Jesus was in the room. As she praised God and thanked him for touching her child, she felt the boy moving in the bed. Several minutes later, when the nurse came to check his condition, she was amazed that his vital signs had returned to normal. Within three weeks he left the hospital and returned to school.

Every situation requires its own unique spiritual direction. The Gospel narratives reveal that Jesus did not follow a set pattern or technique in his healing ministry, but each request for help was treated differently. One paralytic is told to take up his bed and walk, and another is advised his sins are forgiven. Jesus laid his hands on one blind man to restore his sight, and he applied a mixture of mud and spittle to heal another.

It appears that Jesus treated each person as an individual when he responded to his or her needs. This attitude in our prayer intentions will greatly aid our intercessory prayers.

Where Is God?

God, are you real?

The little child whispered,
"God, speak to me,"
And a meadowlark sang.
But the child did not hear.

So the child yelled,
"God, speak to me!"

And the thunder rolled across the sky
But the child did not listen.

The child looked around and said,
"God, let me see you,"
And a star shone brightly
But the child did not notice.

And the child shouted,
"God, show me a miracle!"
And a life was born
But the child did not know.

So the child cried out in despair,
"Touch me, God, and let me know you are here!"
Whereupon God reached down and touched the
child.
But the child brushed the butterfly away
And walked away unknowingly.

Author Unknown

Often times, the things we seek are right underneath our noses. Don't miss out on your blessing because it isn't packaged as you expected.

$\mathscr{H}$ow Should We Pray?

Jesus answered, "Have faith in God. I tell you solemnly, if anyone says to this mountain, 'Get up and throw yourself into the sea,' with no hesitation in his heart but believing that what he says will happen, it will be done for him. I tell you therefore: everything you ask and pray for, believe that you have it already, and it will be yours."

MARK 11:23-25

Jesus gave firm guidelines to his disciples concerning intercessory prayer. This passage from the Gospel of Mark illustrates the attitude of faith he expected from his followers who were seriously seeking answers to their petitions. Years of experience have convinced me that our prayer life will be richly blessed if we follow the rules Jesus laid down. Prayers for physical needs, emotional balance, and spiritual renewal become more effective when we apply these simple principles to our lives.

The Scripture passage above describes Jesus and his friends on the road to Jerusalem. They had traveled this way the previous day when our Lord commanded the barren fig tree, "May no one ever eat fruit from you again (Mk 11;14)." Peter expressed astonishment as he noted the tree had completely withered away during the night. Jesus used the situation to discourse on the power of prayer.

His first direction states, "Have faith in God." The word "faith" can often be a stumbling block to Christians, who may view it as some abstract, spiritual component that somehow adds a magical touch to intercessory prayers. "Claim your healing" ministries exhort people to have faith as they pray over them—and accuse them of a lack of faith if the answer is not forthcoming. This method puts an unfair burden of responsibility upon the person seeking help.

Sometimes the responsibility for believing rests with the person doing the praying rather than the one asking for prayer. The healing of the paralytic in Luke 5:17-26 is such an example. The four friends were unable to maneuver the man on his mat through the crowd. Undaunted, they carried him to the top of the house, where they removed the loose-fitting tiles and lowered him to the feet of Jesus. Seeing their faith he said, "My friend, your sins are forgiven you (v.20)." Perhaps little is said about the faith of the sick man because he was so wounded in body and spirit that he ceased to believe he could be cured. Jesus was able to appropriate the faith of his friends to bring wholeness to the man's life.

We cannot command faith into a person as if it is an attitude that we can change. Faith doesn't demand; it trusts. A helpful analogy is the trapeze artist. He can swing back and forth monotonously for hours if he chooses. But to move on to other things, he must let go of his safe, comfortable bar and hang in mid-air for a moment, trusting that his partner will be there to catch him before he falls to the ground. If the trapeze artist is tumbling in a somersault, he cannot even see if someone is waiting for him; he must blindly let go of his life supports.

Faith isn't a feeling; it's an action. This implies doing something about our beliefs, not merely talking about them. Abraham was willing to sacrifice his son Isaac on the altar, and this is why he is called the "friend of God." The letter of James says of Abraham, "His faith became perfect by what he did" (Jas 2:22-23). Like Abraham's, our relationship with the Father is established through the action of trusting him by putting into practice the tiny "mustard seed" of faith we all possess (see Lk 17:6). Attending church services, reading the Bible, spending time in prayer are all examples of faith in action.

Once when I was leading a healing prayer service in a local church, I was asked to pray for a nine-day-old infant who was diagnosed with apnea, a serious respiratory condition which can sometimes lead to Sudden Infant Death Syndrome (SIDS). The chest of the little boy was attached to a machine that constantly monitored his breathing. A loud buzzer alerted the parents whenever his respirations became abnormal. They told me this was happening twenty or twenty-five times each day and night. Naturally, everyone was stressed and exhausted from the situation.

I invited the five hundred people in the church to join me in praying for the child and his parents. One year later, when I was again ministering in the same parish, the parents came to report their son's complete healing. From the time we prayed, the machine ceased sending out warnings and the baby never had another respiratory crisis. The mother said she was greatly relieved but also felt guilty because she had doubted God's willingness to heal her son. "I came into the church that night with no faith at all," she confessed. She believed faith was a feeling of absolute confidence that the prayers would be answered, "but I was angry, tired, anxious, and fearful." I helped her to understand that she was demonstrating faith when she walked into the church with her son. Her actions clearly indicated a belief in God's power even if her feelings did not.

Whenever we encounter the word *faith* in the Scripture, it's helpful to insert the word "trust" to gain a better understanding of the message. When we trust someone, we believe that person has our best interests at heart. When my five children were small, I often asked a neighbor to watch them while I ran some errands. I knew she would love and care for them just as she did her own children. I didn't repeatedly beg her to keep an eye on them nor did I plead with her to feed them at mealtimes. Such a lack of consideration never entered my mind.

Yet we often approach God with this kind of anxiety and fear. We beg him to see the seriousness of our problems or plead with him for healing of loved ones as if we were attempting to overcome the Father's destructive will. Jesus taught us, "The Son can do nothing by himself; he can do only what he sees the Father doing, and whatever the Father does the Son does too" (Jn 5:19). Jesus is God's definition of himself. The Word became flesh so we could know the true personality of our Creator.

To have "faith in God" means to trust that the Father's

will for us is much more wonderful than we can possibly imagine. A healthy prayer attitude is one of childlike simplicity, believing God wants to answer prayer more than we want to ask.

One of my grandchildren provided me with an excellent example of this kind of attitude. Steven was four years old when his new baby sister was born. One day as I was caring for him, we were looking through his newest book. It contained no words, just pictures. The child was to use his imagination to concoct a story to go with the pictures.

We turned to a page that showed a young boy with a baseball bat in his hands. In the distance was a house with a broken window, and running toward the boy was a man with his arms raised. Steven said, "The little boy got a ball and bat for his birthday. He could hit the ball really far and it broke a window in his house."

"Who is this man?" I asked.

"That's his Daddy. He's going to pick him up and tell him, 'It's OK, don't cry, I can fix it.'" Developing this kind of trust in God can greatly aid our prayers.

The next maxim set forth in the teaching of Jesus begins, "If anyone says to this mountain, 'Get up and throw yourself into the sea ...'" (Mk 11:23). It's helpful to note that Jesus doesn't ask us to ask the Father in heaven to speak to the mountain. The authority for moving the mountain rests within us. This recalls the account of creation in the book of Genesis: "God blessed them, saying to them, 'Be fruitful, multiply, fill the earth and conquer it. Be masters of the fish of the sea, the birds of heaven and all living animals upon the earth'" (Gn 1:28).

As the highest form of life on earth, humankind was given by God dominion over all creation. Thus we have the authority to pray when threatened by the forces of nature: hurricanes, earthquakes, tornadoes, and so on. Jesus did this to the fig tree and he expects us to follow his example whenever we encounter disaster.

Perhaps we will never be in a position to need to move a mountain, but we can exercise such authority in other ways. Occasionally I have asked for guidance when praying for a sick person and received the impression to command the illness to depart, and it has complied. Just as Jesus rebuked the fever of Peter's mother-in-law and she got up from her bed (see Mt 8:14-15), so we are sometimes guided to take authority over sickness.

One evening after we had begun holding weekly prayer meetings in our homes, a young woman requested prayer prior to undergoing surgery for a lump in the breast. We asked Jesus to surround the anxiety she was experiencing. Then we spoke to the cells in her body that were not acting in a healthy, creative manner and told them to stop their erratic behavior. The lump disappeared almost immediately and, after he examined her, her doctor canceled the surgery.

When our son, Steve, was eight years old, he fell from the upper bunk of his bed and lay on the floor, screaming with pain in his right arm. The X rays showed a pathological fracture of his arm. Our physician said it was not caused by the fall but due to an unusually large bone cyst that apparently had been developing for quite some time. The cyst, growing inside the bone of his upper arm, had reduced it to the fragility of an eggshell.

Two orthopedic specialists who examined Steve impressed us with the seriousness of his condition. One said it was the largest bone cyst he had ever seen. They told us he would be in a cast from his neck to his waist for at least six months, then in an arm sling for another extended period. We were advised to "teach him how to play chess" because any type of contact sport would aggravate the condition.

Our prayer group prayed over Steve, asking Jesus to accelerate this healing process. We encouraged him to speak to the cells in his arm, asking them to fill in the empty spaces. We also encouraged him to "see himself well," running down the basketball court and making baskets.

After six weeks, the cast was removed and an X ray taken to determine proper alignment. Our physician seemed somewhat incredulous as he compared the latest X rays to the originals. He could find no evidence of a fracture or a bone cyst. When I asked about limiting Steve's activity, he replied, "A kid that heals that fast can do anything he wants." Steve grew up to be an exceptionally talented high school basketball player.

Perhaps speaking to a mountain isn't so far-fetched after all. Living in California and Florida has given me ample opportunity to speak to hurricanes and earthquakes when there are dire predictions of disaster. Often the earth under our feet has stopped shifting or the winds have decreased in intensity. Once, as strong thunderstorms and tornadoes approached an outdoor Mass and healing service at the rodeo arena in Billings, Montana, we were told to evacuate the area immediately. Instead, we said a prayer asking the winds to blow softly and the rain to fall gently. Since most of the participants were spending the night in tents and RVs, we prayed for a quiet, peace-filled night. The next day we were told the tornadoes changed course just outside the rodeo arena, producing only a slight drizzle during the night.

Jesus also teaches us, "Everything you ask and pray for, believe you have it already and it will be yours" (Mk 11:25).

How can we demonstrate such a belief when we see suffering, hopelessness, and despair in a situation? We are asked to believe in our hearts, not our heads. This is the portion of the prayer of faith inviting us to use creative imagination.

We live in a culture demanding rational explanations to confirm every phenomenon, making it difficult to rely on intuitive promptings. Six months after the disastrous earthquake rocked Oakland, California, in October, 1989, I was asked to lead a day of prayer for dozens of local residents still suffering the effects of emotional shock. Nearly three quarters of the participants reported having received warnings of an earthquake in dreams, Scripture, and prophetic messages just prior to that fateful day. Yet most chose to disregard these insights rather than pray for protection.

The use of imagination in prayer can aid us in believing we have what we ask already. Some years ago *The New York Times* interviewed Dr. Walter Chase, the director of research and head of the department of basic and visual science at the Southern California College of Optometry in Fullerton. Dr. Chase noted how he teaches his students that there is no physiological difference between the signals activated by the mind's eye and the ones activated by the eye itself. He states, "The things one sees in the mind's eye are as real as those one sees through a window."

His research shows the same physical mechanisms are at work when we think we "see" something happen and when we are actually viewing the event. Many athletes and actors utilize these findings by visualizing a positive performance prior to the real experience. Imagination is not a passive component of our being; it can become an integral part of our prayer life.

When the Holy Spirit guides me to pray for someone who is ill, I picture Jesus touching the person, bringing health and wholeness. I express gratitude for restoration even when there is not yet any evidence of divine intervention. I continue to hold this image of wellness in my mind until it becomes a reality, praising God for his compassionate care.

A woman once asked me to pray for her father, who was dying of emphysema. After I explained this method of believing prayer, she understood the concept but had great difficulty using her imagination. She solved the dilemma by using a photo of her dad taken when he was strong and healthy. She placed the picture above the kitchen sink and, as she washed the dishes, would thank Jesus for healing her father's body, mind, and spirit. He was soon able to leave the hospital and return to work.

The letter to the Hebrews describes the process: "Faith ... can prove the existence of the realities that at present remain unseen" (Heb 11:1). God's power can become activated when we cease wishing for an answer and begin believing he is already at work.

The Reverend Charles L. Kaldahl, the pastor of St. Timothy's Healing Community in Daly City, California, is a prime example of this type of belief. Diagnosed with cancer of the prostate, he was told radiation could be effective against the invader. For thirty-seven days he endured the effects of the procedure when seventy thousand rad units were sent through his pelvic region: unrelenting pain, diarrhea, constipation, sleeplessness, and crazy dreams.

Charles chose to approach the treatment with spiritual creativity. "The radiation machine was immense," he said. "Overhead on the ceiling was taped a cross, a mark placed there to line up the patient with the radiation beam correctly. It wasn't intended to be, but for me it was the cross of Jesus. As I lay there being radiated, I silently spoke the words of the Jesus Prayer, 'Lord Jesus Christ, Son of God, have mercy on me, a sinner.' The technicians came in and out of the room, moving equipment into place, but I would lie there for those fifteen minutes in the deep rest of contemplation on the gift of life for me from the cross."

Charles continued to describe his experience after the treatment:

I needed to drink three to four quarts of water a day to help my body cleanse away the destroyed cells. This water regimen kept me close to the bathroom. One of my friends suggested I put holy pictures in the bathroom so that each trip would be a "pilgrimage."

"Everything I experienced through the radiation process that weakened me for two months gave me greater respect for the many cancer patients I have counseled in various support groups. There is a commendable courage present in the cancer patient. To go each day to face the radiation or the chemotherapy takes a special gift of willpower and determined survival. I was continuously encouraged by the letters, prayers, phone calls and visits of my friends. It constantly reminded me of how much I am loved and how many want me to be well.

Throughout the months of December and January, Charles continued his spiritual and clinical odyssey. He and his faith-filled wife, Jean, were able truly to rejoice on Easter Sunday when his test returns no longer showed any evidence of prostate cancer. "It is Resurrection time for me!" he exclaims. "Every morning comes the Resurrection time."*

---

*Story used by permission of the author, the Reverend Charles L. Kaldahl, director of St. Timothy's Healing Community, Daly City, California.]

This illustration is an excellent example of prayer being answered through the best of medical attention along with consistent spiritual recourse. Using modern medicine, therapy and surgery doesn't suggest a lack of faith but a willingness to couple the achievements of modern medicine with the spiritual power of God's healing love.

I ministered to a woman who had undergone a double mastectomy and was now scheduled to receive six weeks of aggressive chemotherapy sessions. Each morning she phoned me and we would pray for the light of Jesus to surround her, filtering out all harmful chemicals and permitting only life-giving substances to flow through her body. She never experienced the usual side effects of hair loss, nausea, and weight loss. She was able to continue her job during that entire time and has remained cancer-free for several years.

Sometimes a person's illness requires prayer on a regular and consistent basis. Those with chronic or life-threatening illnesses may need frequent "soaking" prayer by family, friends, or prayer team members before they begin to notice changes in their condition.

Some Christians believe it demonstrates a lack of faith to pray more than once for a person. However, Jesus displayed no such reservation when he laid hands on a blind man and then asked, "Can you see anything?" The man, who was beginning to see, replied, "I can see people; they look like trees to me, but they are walking about." Then Jesus laid hands on him a second time, causing him to see everything "plainly and distinctly" (Mk 8:22-26).

I often refer to "soaking prayer" as the W.O.W. Prayer. "W.O.W." stands for "With**O**ut **W**ords" because it's not necessary to say lengthy prayers when praying with someone on a consistent basis. Generally I teach those who are doing the praying to invite the person to relax and quietly receive God's healing power as they gently lay on hands. I instruct them to ask the Holy Spirit silently to bathe the person in the light of his love. If possible, it's helpful to play meditative music in the background. This type of prayer can last for many minutes and can be done several times a day or once a week depending on the situation. Some prayer groups designate time for soaking prayer during each prayer meeting.

It's also important to instruct people to pray over their medications before taking them. Most Christians would never partake of a meal without asking God's blessings on the food, yet they ingest all types of medicinal pills and liquids without ever doing the same. A pharmacologist told me that when he was dispensing pain medication he routinely prayed a blessing over it. Frequently his customers reported much more effectiveness from the prescribed medication even when it was the same dosage.

Suggested Prayer for Medication

Make the sign of the Cross over the medication and say, "In the Name of the Father and of the Son and of the Holy Spirit, I ask that this medicine be blessed with the creative power of God. Please remove any side effects from it that could be detrimental to my physical, emotional or spiritual well-being. Increase the medicine's effectiveness so it may produce healing, restoration, and renewal for my body, mind, and spirit. Amen."

* * *

Wonderful healing blessings are available to us when we humbly stand before the throne of God and ask his merciful love to rain down upon us.

The following prayer is an example of positive intercessory prayer that can be adapted for yourself or others.

Prayer of Healing

Dear Jesus, I believe you have
designed and created me
therefore you can also
repair and restore me.
In the comfort of your love
I pour out to you
the memories that haunt me,
the anxieties that perplex me,
the fears that stifle me,
and the sickness that prevails upon me.
I confess my frustration
in dealing with the
emotional, physical, and
spiritual pain of my life.
Help me envision
your gentle touch
upon my being
as you tenderly
enclose me in your arms.
Give me inner sight
to see you companioning me
every step of my earthly journey.
I trust your tender care will

yield peace to my mind,
serenity to my heart,
renewal to my spirit, and
healing to my body.
For all the ways you are
already answering my prayers,
I give you praise and thanksgiving. Amen.

Chapter Four

Forgiveness

I give you a new commandment: love one another;
just as I have loved you.

JOHN 13:34

Jesus did not merely suggest we were to love one another; he made it a new commandment. Jesus demonstrated a love that encompassed everyone, even his enemies. He denounced the scribes and Pharisees in his teachings but did not exclude them from the benefits of his redemptive act. In the midst of the agonizing suffering of his crucifixion he prayed for his persecutors, "Father, forgive them; they do not know what they are doing" (Lk 23:34). He had the power to retaliate by calling on the angels to avenge him, yet he chose the path of forgiveness.

Being angry over unjust and unfair treatment is a normal and healthy response to pain. St. Paul's counsel to the church at Ephesus, "Even if you are angry, you must not sin" (Eph 4:26), is a piece of advice containing much wisdom. Anger is our best defense against injustice when it is used as a constructive emotion to correct wrongs. But if it is used to harm others in an effort to "get even," it can become a source of sin in our lives.

For healthy spiritual growth, it's important to feel the emotions associated with the painful episodes of life. Many Christians try to skip over uncomfortable feelings by jumping into forgiveness too soon. They mistakenly believe it is their "Christian" duty to keep the peace by pretending everything is fine. Thus it's possible to repress, avoid, or ignore much of what may need to be remedied.

A woman attending one of my retreats asked for prayer because she was very depressed and her consumption of alcohol had become uncontrollable. I suggested it would be a step toward wellness to explore her feelings toward a neighbor who had wrongly accused her son of sexual misconduct. She refused by insisting she had forgiven the other person and it was no longer a problem. Her unwillingness to admit honestly her feelings of hurt, disappointment, or rejection made it difficult to seek God's healing for these wounds.

In the other extreme, it is possible never to let go of the desire to get even. Such a person almost delights in wallowing in self-pity and endless recounting of the list of offenses. He or she prefers to remain full of bitterness, believing such "righteous indignation" is appropriate for the pain that was suffered.

At some point the wronged individual needs to make a conscious decision to forgive. Forgiveness is a decision, not a feeling. We don't necessarily feel warm, loving, or generous, but it is possible to decide to cease clutching the pain and let it go.

We cannot always control what happens to us, but we can control our reaction to the happenings. We can refuse to allow victimization by another person to break our spirit, make us physically ill, or interfere with our spiritual growth. Most physicians suspect that anger, worry and stress can make us sicker than a virus. The Chinese have a way of saying it: "You cannot stop the birds of worry from flying over your head, but you can prevent them from making a nest in your hair." Bitterness is like an acid. It can do more harm to the container in which it is stored than to the object on which it is poured.

A lack of forgiveness can often impede our ability to pray for ourselves or for others. It can act like an invisible barrier prohibiting us from the graces and blessings we are seeking. Jesus taught us, "When you stand in prayer, forgive whatever you have against anybody, so that your Father in heaven may forgive your failings too" (Mk 11:25). We cannot receive the fullness of God's love for ourselves or others if we refuse to forgive those who have wronged us.

I once prayed with a woman suffering with a chronic bladder infection. She had sought relief through many forms of medication and received ministry from her prayer group, but the discomfort persisted. I asked the Holy Spirit for guidance regarding her situation, and felt led to ask, "What are you trying to eliminate in your life?" She described her past as "being in hell" after her husband deserted the family, leaving her the sole support of three young children. She expressed much bitterness and rage toward her former spouse. "I'm trying to eliminate him!" she sobbed.

We talked about her feelings and spent time praying for the wounds in her heart. I suggested she go into the chapel and honestly admit to God all that she was carrying within her. Several days later, after much soul-searching, she again asked me to pray. She had gradually come to realize the hatred was hurting her far more than it was punishing him. I invited her to pray a blessing prayer for him; then, we asked God to touch her body and heal it. Several weeks later I received a letter stating the physical symptoms had disappeared and she was experiencing newfound freedom in her life.

We may have to practice the "discipline of forgiveness"

on a consistent basis if we live or work with someone who makes life miserable for us. This does not mean passive acceptance of abuse, but a willingness to renounce vengeance and retaliation.

As I began to comprehend the beneficial effects of prayer on the recovery of my patients, I spent an increased amount of time ministering to their spiritual needs. This was a source of displeasure to some of my coworkers. One doctor in particular gave me a hard time and availed himself of every opportunity to chide me for "getting religion." We had been close friends and, since he was unable to understand the changes in me, he resorted to sarcastic remarks that deeply wounded me.

The simplest way of dealing with the situation was to avoid him whenever possible, but I realized this was not a solution. So I began applying the forgiving love of Jesus Christ whenever we had an encounter. The prayer in my heart was, "Lord, I forgive him for his hurting words. Let me see him as you see him and love him as you love him." Gradually our relationship became less strained and the heckling stopped.

Extending the hand of forgiveness can be a process requiring small steps toward wholeness. Sometimes the most we can do is pray, "Father, help me to be willing to be willing to forgive the person who wounded me." Such a half-step begins to open a spiritual door, allowing God's graces to flow. When we no longer desire to punish the other person, forgiveness has begun.

Sometimes we are hesitant to forgive because we don't want to return to an abusive situation. It's important to note the difference between forgiveness and reconciliation. Jesus taught us to forgive others the wrongs done to us, but he did not mandate reconciliation. Reconciliation necessitates an earnest desire on the part of both individuals to do whatever it takes to live in harmony with one another. This may be an impossible feat where there is an unwillingness to work on the relationship problems. Forgiveness doesn't guarantee or expect a change in another's behavior, but it does promise to bring new spiritual blessings to the one who practices it.

It is also important to ask for forgiveness when we have offended others. For several weeks we received no answers to our prayers for a woman who was trying to find employment. She was the sole support for her teenage children and their financial situation was becoming desperate. One evening, as we were again praying with her, someone asked if she could recall anything which might be a block to the situation. Was there a person she needed to forgive, or, perhaps, someone who needed to forgive her?

She remembered her former employer had fired her because she gossiped about him to the office staff. There had been many hurt feelings and no effort made to mend the relationship. Early the next morning, she walked into the man's office and apologized for her thoughtless behavior. He was understandably puzzled by the unexpected visit, and was surprised to discover that she was not merely attempting to regain her former position. A few hours later, she received a phone call informing her that a previous job application had been accepted.

Unwillingness to ask for forgiveness can erect strong barriers against God's ability to bring blessings. A newspaper article told of two brothers in Massachusetts who died within hours of one another. For twenty-five years they had split the family with a feud caused by a long-forgotten disagreement. The feud ended when they both died of heart attacks in the same emergency room with the same physician on the same day. The bitterness against one another had been so great it prevented them from visiting their ailing mother because neither wanted to encounter the other at her bedside. They died without ever reconciling the situation, leaving brokenness and sorrow in their households.

Jesus frequently reminded his disciples that forgiving others was a condition of being a true follower of his.

Peter needed clarification. "'How often must I forgive my brother if he wrongs me? As often as seven times?' Jesus answered, 'Not seven I tell you, but seventy-seven times'" (Mt 18:21-22). Peter wanted a specific number, but Jesus responded with a deliberately inflated figure denoting an infinite amount because forgiveness is never-ending if we truly desire fellowship with the Father.

The need to forgive and be forgiven also extends to our relationship with God. It is not uncommon to become upset with the Deity, as illustrated by many scriptural passages. Moses cried out against God, "Why do you treat your servant so badly? Why have I not found favor with you, so that you load on me the weight of all this nation? ... If this is how you want to deal with me, I would rather you killed me!" (Num 11:11, 15).

Several of the psalms also express similar discontent with Divine Providence. "How much longer will you forget me, Yahweh? Forever? How much longer will you hide your face from me? How much longer must I endure grief in my soul and sorrow in my heart by day and by night?" (Ps 13:1-2). I believe these passages represent honest feelings of powerlessness regarding our human existence. It's been rightly noted that we are not human beings striving to be spiritual but spiritual beings trying to be human. Prayerfully expressing our frustrations toward God doesn't diminish his love for us. However, deep resentment and bitterness can be a block to grace.

I once cared for a man who was furious with the Lord. "God killed my son," he insisted, "in an auto accident." For many years he refused to go to church or permit anyone in his family to discuss religion. He was hospitalized in the terminal stage of colon cancer. Each day as I attended to his physical needs, I'd silently pray for the Lord to touch his broken heart. On the night before he died, he consented to a visit from the hospital chaplain. Later, he tearfully told his wife, "Honey, I feel such peace. Why didn't I do this years ago?"

During his agony on the cross, Jesus demonstrated the importance of forgiveness when he cried, "Father, forgive them, they do not know what they are doing" (Lk 23:24). In the midst of excruciating pain, he looked at the crowd demanding his crucifixion and refused to allow resentment and bitterness into his heart. There may have been many in that group who had received healings from Jesus and had listened to his teachings, yet they were caught up in the mob mentality. Jesus had the power to retaliate by summoning legions of angels to avenge him, but he chose the way of forgiveness.

Learning to walk in the Father's love, trusting him to care for our daily needs, means frequently examining our hearts to see if we are harboring grudges, hurt feelings, or a desire for revenge.

Prayer for Grace to Forgive

"God, examine me and know my heart, probe me and know my thoughts" (Ps 139:23). Thank you for the many times you have forgiven my failings and help me to do the same toward others. Illuminate my inner being with the light of your Holy Spirit to reveal any need to forgive or to be forgiven. Grant me the grace to say, "I'm sorry," to anyone I may have wounded by my words or actions. Help me to uncover hidden areas of bitterness within my heart. I desire to forgive those who have hurt me and ask you to bless them wherever they may be. Let me recall your words from the cross, "Father, forgive them for they do not know what they are doing," and echo them in my own life. Heal me of the memories of harmful words and actions so I no longer carry them within me. Father, I also seek to let go of any anger I have held against you. I cannot always understand your ways, but I believe you want only the best for me and my loved ones. Bestow from your abundance the gift of love for myself and for others. Amen.

Chapter Five

Grief and Loss

There is a season for everything ... a time for giving birth, a time for dying.

ECCLESIASTES 3:1-2

How do we pray for others when it seems their physical bodies are not being healed? When do we cease asking for healing and begin praying for the grace of a gentle death?

The book of Hebrews tells us that all "must die once, and after that the judgment"(Heb 9:28). Even Lazarus, whom Jesus miraculously brought back to life, eventually succumbed to the process we call death. For each of us there will come a time when our earthly journey is complete. Death was the final enemy to be overcome through the resurrected body of Jesus Christ. Therefore, praying for healing means we always pray for wholeness of body, mind, and spirit. But we must also recognize the imperfection of this earthly world. When Jesus returns to establish his kingdom, "there will be no more death, and no more mourning or sadness. The world of the past [will be] gone" (Rv 21:4).

When I embarked on my quest to learn how to pray for others, I wanted to believe that everyone would be healed in the here and now if the correct principles of faith were applied. As a nurse, I was accustomed to using a procedure manual as a guide for successful patient care. I viewed the Bible as a similar source of information. I set about studying the teachings of Jesus and was somewhat frustrated to discover no clear rules regarding healing prayer. He didn't practice a standard technique but sought the Father's will for each person. Prayers for others must always take into consideration our human limitations since we cannot fully comprehend the work of God.

In the early stages of learning how to pray, I recall being devastated when a young mother died of uterine cancer. Our prayer group had spent many hours in prayer and fasting for her. I blamed myself for not having enough faith. I was angry at God for his failure to answer the prayer in the way I anticipated. Our prayer group had received numerous Scripture passages and prophetic messages encouraging us to pray and she would be healed. Why did it turn out this way? It took me a long time to grasp this truth: healing prayer must always encompass the possibility of physical death. Christ said that believers "will lay their hands on the sick, who will recover" (Mk 16:18), but recovery may only be complete when we return to the arms of the Father.

In 1993, my seventy-six-year-old mother was diagnosed with cancer of the kidney. She underwent successful removal of her right kidney but her remaining kidney was nonfunctioning, necessitating dialysis. She frequently expressed a desire to die. My father had already passed on and she was prepared to meet Jesus. Each day we prayed together for the healing touch of Jesus to bless her in body, mind, and spirit. Six weeks after her surgery, the nonfunctioning kidney began to perform and she was taken off dialysis. This close encounter with death seemed to inspire my mother with a determination to live each day to the fullest. She sold the house she had inhabited for nearly fifty years and bought a new one. She learned to drive a car and was as excited as a teen-ager in showing off her first driver's license. For six years she was full of life, until the cancer invaded her brain. This time the prayers for healing did not end in earthly restoration.

On the night she died, my sister Pam and I were quietly sitting on Mom's front porch when our conversation was abruptly interrupted by a visit from a tiny, fluttering hummingbird. It gracefully flew around our heads for several minutes. Pam remarked that she'd never seen a hummingbird in Mom's yard and wasn't it unusual to see one at 9:30 in the evening? We watched her as she flew to the bright, yellow lilies planted in front of the porch. After retrieving some of the nectar, she once more circled our heads before soundlessly flying away.

We pondered this incident as we kept watch with Mom throughout the night, stroking her hair and her hands, telling her we loved her. At 3:30 A.M., we decided to pray the rosary together. It seemed like an appropriate prayer because, in spite of being a lifelong member of the Methodist Church, Mom had often demonstrated devotion to Mary, the Mother of Jesus.

When I was in grammar school, I recall her helping me construct a crepe paper Marian grotto, which was prominently displayed in our dining room during the entire month of May. She encouraged me to keep fresh flowers in a small vase near Mary's statue. For several years, she regularly attended a ceramic class where she chose to make each of her five children a ceramic wall hanging of Mary as Queen of Heaven.

As we completed our prayers, a feeling of deep peace and tender love seemed to permeate the bedroom.

Mom's breathing was no longer labored and she quietly took her last breath. We remained next to her for a long time, weeping with a mixture of sorrow and gratitude. Later that morning, Pam reminded me of the hummingbird's appearance. "I think that was symbolic of Mom's spirit," she said. "Toward the end of her life she resembled a very tiny hummingbird as she flitted from room to room, chair to chair, subject to subject, whenever we were with her." God truly sent us a messenger of "hope" in that little bird so we would know our prayers for healing had been answered. Her earthly journey was over and we believed she now resided in a place where pain could not reach her.

When praying for an elderly individual, it isn't unusual to consider the possibility of death. Healing prayers for a baby, a child, or a young person are another matter. The following story sent to me by a physician illustrates such a dilemma.

A Little Boy's Heart

The surgeon sat beside the boy's bed; the boy's parents sat across from him. "Tomorrow morning," the surgeon began, "I'll open up your heart ..."

"You'll find Jesus there," the boy interrupted.

The surgeon looked up, annoyed. "I'll cut your heart open," he continued, "to see how much damage has been done ..."

"But when you open up my heart, you'll find Jesus in there."

The surgeon looked to the parents, who sat quietly. "When I see how much damage has been done, I'll sew your heart and chest back up and I'll plan what to do next."

"But you'll find Jesus in my heart. The Bible says he lives there. The hymns all say he lives there. You'll find him in my heart."

The surgeon had had enough. "I'll tell you what I'll find in your heart. I'll find damaged muscle, low blood supply, and weakened vessels. And I'll find out if I can make you well."

"You'll find Jesus there, too. He lives there."

The surgeon left. Following the surgery he sat in his office, recording his notes from the surgery: "*Damaged aorta, damaged pulmonary vein, widespread muscle degeneration. No hope for transplant, no hope for cure. Therapy: painkillers and bedrest. Prognosis...*" Here he paused. "*Death within one year.*"

He stopped the recorder, but there was more to

be said. "Why?" he asked aloud. "Why did you do this? You've put him here; you've put him in this pain and you've cursed him to an early death. Why?"

The Lord answered and said, "The boy, my lamb, was not meant for your flock for long, for he is a part of my flock and will forever be. Here, in my flock, he will feel no pain, and will be comforted as you cannot imagine. His parents will one day join him here, and they will know peace, and my flock will continue to grow."

The surgeon's tears were hot, but his anger was hotter. "You created that boy, and you created that heart. He'll be dead in months. Why?"

The Lord answered, "The boy, my lamb, shall return to my flock, for he has done his duty. I did not put my lamb with your flock to lose him, but to retrieve another lost lamb." The surgeon wept.

The surgeon sat beside the boy's bed; the boy's parents sat across from him.

The boy awoke and whispered, "Did you cut open my heart?"

"Yes," said the surgeon.

"What did you find?" asked the boy.

"I found Jesus there," said the surgeon.

The Jews have a saying: "Death doesn't take the old but the ripe." Healing prayer is a petition asking God to do the most loving thing for someone. After my mother's death, I found the following handwritten poem in her Bible. During her life she had experienced four miscarriages and the death of a three-day-old son. She knew the pain of losing a little one.

Little Angels

When God calls little children to dwell with him above,
We mortals sometime question the wisdom of his love.
Perhaps God tires of calling the aged to his fold,
So he picks a rosebud before it can grow old.
God knows how much we need them,
and so he takes but few,
To make the land of heaven more beautiful to view.
Believing this is difficult, still somehow we must try.
The saddest word mankind knows
Will always be "Goodbye."
So when a little child departs, we who are left behind
Must realize God loves children; angels are hard to find.

Author Unknown

* * *

Seeking complete healing for ourselves and others is the responsibility of each Christian. Such intercessions imply surrendering all to God and trusting in his mercy. One day, we will fully understand. "Now we are seeing a dim reflection in a mirror; but then we shall be seeing face to face. The knowledge that I have now is imperfect; but then I shall know as fully as I am known" (1 Cor 13:12).

Prayer for Healing of Body and Soul

Dear Father, I pray for _____ to be restored in body, mind and spirit. His/her physical body appears to be deteriorating but death cannot destroy the spirit. Let the light of your love continue to illuminate any past memories in need of healing. May your mercy bring consolation to his/her heart, as you replace fear with trust in your tender care. Grant the grace of reconciliation for any relationships that need mending. Bless all friends and family members with the gift of peace as they release this loved one into your care. Through the victory of the cross of Jesus Christ, I trust that he/she will never truly die, but will live eternally in your embrace. Amen.

* * *

Chapter Six

Inner Healing

Out of his infinite glory, may he give you the power through his Spirit for your hidden self to grow strong, so that Christ may live in your hearts through faith.

EPHESIANS 3:16-17

Physical healing may sometimes be delayed or obstructed by psychological barriers. Memories of pain and sorrow, experiences of rejection and loss, episodes of abuse and neglect can exact a heavy toll on our bodies. There is much scientific data pointing to the body-mind connection as a source of illness. Physicians estimate that eighty percent of the patients they treat are suffering psychosomatic problems. I well remember one of my nursing school instructors asking, "What is the cause of all disease?" We ventured several answers: Microorganisms? Pollutants? He replied, "All disease is ultimately caused by the wear and tear of the soul on the body."

One physician told me he routinely seeks to learn what was happening in the emotional life of his seriously ill patients when they first noted symptoms of their condition. He calls this "returning to the scene of the crime," because it often elicits helpful information for subsequent treatment. He sometimes suggests counseling with a qualified therapist to complement his care for their physical bodies.

I recall praying for a man who had undergone bypass surgery for his heart. Following the procedure he underwent a succession of complications that seriously affected his convalescence. His family and the local intercessory prayer group were faithfully interceding but the situation was becoming grave. I spent time talking with his wife and discovered he had lost his job a few weeks prior to the onset of heart problems. She said, "It nearly broke his heart after being with the firm for so many years." I suggested she pray with him for inner healing, asking Jesus to set him free from the feelings of rejection and loss. Several weeks later I received a letter detailing his return to health and describing his satisfaction with a new job.

The body-mind connection can often explain irrational fears that sometimes upset our lives. One woman requested prayer because she had an inordinate fear of the outdoors. She was a highly educated person who ran her own business, yet she could not be outside for any length of time without feeling severe anxiety. This greatly curtailed her ability to enjoy a vacation with her husband and children. In our prayer, we asked the Lord to touch anything in her past that may have provoked such behavior, and a rather simple episode came to her mind.

As a small child she was playing along the bank of a river and, oblivious to the dangers of the rushing water, began to wade into it. Suddenly, she became aware of shouts of alarm as her father scooped her into his arms, warning her never to go near the water again. Although many years had gone by, the intensity of that command continued to affect her life. I invited her to recreate the scene in her imagination, this time bringing Jesus into the picture. She was to imagine the Lord walking with her along the riverbank, pointing out the beauty of his Father's creation. It was obvious that she had been freed from fear when, several months later, a postcard arrived from the Grand Canyon describing the marvelous time she and her family were having at the park.

Are we merely dealing with the power of suggestion when praying for inner healing for one another? While autosuggestion may be a factor, praying with infants and children has convinced me there is a more potent power at work. At one time, we lived next to a family who had just adopted a one-week-old infant. The adoptive parents were concerned because the baby seemed to repulse their attempts to cuddle him. He also began to demonstrate physical problems that were diagnosed as pyloric stenosis: a nonfunctioning valve at the end of the esophagus was keeping food from entering the stomach. Surgery was scheduled when I was asked to pray with the little boy.

I remember entering the pediatric ward and seeing his pale skin and the dark circles around his eyes. He was a very sick baby as his mother and I prayed for him. We knew the birth mother was a young, unwed woman so we asked Jesus to free the infant from any feelings of anxiety, shame, or guilt that may have entered into him during the prenatal period. Modern psychiatry acknowledges that the infant in the womb is susceptible to strong maternal feelings that may affect healthy development. As we prayed, there were visible changes in the baby's condition. His skin lost its pallor; his breathing became less labored. Subsequently the surgery was canceled when the baby began taking a bottle with no adverse affects. The prayer also produced an added bonus. He no longer resisted being cuddled by his parents. Today, many years later, he is a successful businessman with children of his own.

Isaiah prophesied, "Ours were the sufferings he bore, ours the sorrows he carried ... on him lies a punishment that brings us peace, and through his wounds we are healed" (Is 53:4-5). Most Christians acknowledge the truth that Jesus died to forgive the sins we knowingly committed. Few realize he also took to the cross the sins committed against us. Anything causing us sorrow, suffering, or emotional distress was transformed through his saving grace. His resurrected presence brought light into the darkness of the whole earth and also into the shadow areas of our minds.

Sometimes memories are so deeply buried we no longer recognize their effect. Psychologists frequently use the illustration of an iceberg in describing the human mind. The small portion above the water's surface compares to the conscious mind, which houses the mechanisms of our present awareness. However, it would be impossible to remain fully conscious of every aspect of our lives, so the unconscious mind, nearly ninety percent, is the repository of everything that has ever happened to us.

Good memories can be brought to consciousness without too much difficulty, but traumatic episodes are often suppressed into deep mental recesses as we attempt to forget the emotional pain associated with them. Unfortunately, we cannot escape one of the primary characteristics of the unconscious: like an elephant it never forgets anything. The unhealed hurts continue to abide within us. Occasionally, when experiencing periods of stress, we may lose control of our ability to suppress all those feelings and we "overreact," "flip our lid," or "blow our cool." Such terminology is beautifully descriptive of the mechanism involved, since something with much energy has been released from within.

Persons reared in families with mental or physical abuse usually have little trouble identifying their need for inner healing. But what about those who belong to basically good families where parents tried their best to care for them? Does everyone need this type of prayer? Many years of experience in healing prayer ministry has convinced me everyone is in some way bound by chains of the past. Since no human being can ever love us perfectly, it may be hard for some of us to believe that we are perfectly lovable. Everyone has encountered some type of rejection or loss that may block emotional, spiritual, or physical wellness.

St. Paul's epistle to the Romans contains a vivid description of this type of mental conflict. "I cannot understand my own behavior. I fail to carry out the things I want to do, and I find myself doing the very things I hate ... my body follows a different law that battles against the law which my reason dictates.... Who will rescue me from this body doomed to death?" (Rom 7:15; 23-24). Paul's dilemma is resolved as he recognizes Jesus as the answer to all the needs of human imperfections.

Is faith in Jesus Christ sufficient to meet all of our inner needs? We do become spiritually healed when we accept Jesus as our Savior. Salvation and eternal life are secured through his death and resurrection. However, we can commit to the Lord only those parts of our lives consciously available to us. The regions of the unconscious, below the level of our awareness, are not always readily accessible. The hidden self may be concealed, requiring us willingly to invite the Holy Spirit to cleanse and set free our entire being.

The following prayer meditation is designed to bring God's merciful touch into the deep mind. Find a place where you can be quiet and uninterrupted. Come before the Lord in an attitude of humility and trust.

Prayer for Inner Healing

Jesus, I invite you to enter my heart and touch those life experiences in need of healing. Bring your love to every corner of my being. Enlighten the shadowy places with your Holy Spirit. Walk back through my life to the very moment when I was conceived. Cleanse my bloodlines and free me from those things which may be exerting a negative influence. Bless me as I was being formed within my mother's womb and remove all barriers to wholeness that may have affected me during those months of gestation. For this I give you thanks.

Heal any physical or emotional trauma that may have harmed me during the birth process. Thank you, Jesus, for being there to receive me into your arms at the very moment of my birth. Breathe your life into my lungs as I take my first breath. In that moment, consecrate me as a child of God and let me always know your saving graces.

Jesus, I praise you for the early months of my infancy. Perhaps there were moments when I needed my mother's tender touch and she was unavailable or unable to do so. Bring your mother, Mary, to fill in the empty places as she holds me, rocks me, and sings to me the way she did for you. Fill in those parts of my being that may have needed more of a father's protection and strength.

Let me know a "daddy" who will ever watch over me with vigilance and care.

Heal me of hurts arising from relationships within my family. Bring peace to my heart if there was a brother or sister, aunt or uncle, grandparent or other relative who treated me with unkindness or cruelty. Perhaps my early childhood was marked by the death of someone close to me. Please heal my heart of any lingering effects of grief or sorrow.

I also pray for a healing of those years spent in the classroom. The actions of classmates and teachers may have caused me to erect a shell around my heart in order to avoid further hurt. Maybe I became shy and uncomfortable in groups due to ridicule or criticism experienced in school. Perhaps I've gone through life thinking I was stupid because of unrecognized learning difficulties. Jesus, let me perceive you sitting next to me at my desk, taking away the fear and granting renewed confidence in my own abilities.

Lord, adolescence brought experiences that confused, frightened, or embarrassed me. Enter my heart and take from me all the memories of negative experiences in my teen years. Let me remember this period of my life without feelings of shame or remorse.

Father, "it was you who created my inmost self, and put

me together in my mother's womb; for all these mysteries I thank you: for the wonder of myself, for the wonder of your works" (Ps 139:13-14). Amen.

Chapter Seven

Discernment

If there is any one of you who needs wisdom, he must ask God, who gives to all freely and ungrudgingly; it will be given to him.

JAMES 1:5

Discernment is a fascinating subject. Properly done it can broaden our horizons, challenge our faith, raise our hopes, and allay our fears. We all want to understand how to discern, and how to know God's will. We want to learn the secret of truly knowing God's perfect will in every situation.

What prayer shall I say and when shall I say it? How do I listen for the voice of God? How does God speak? How do I determine when a message is from God or from my own thoughts?

We spend a great deal of time and energy seeking to know what God wants us to do, and we're not always certain our hunches are right. A boy was watching his father, a Protestant minister, write his Sunday sermon. "How do you know what to say?" he asked.

"Why, God tells me," the clergyman replied.

"Oh," said the boy. "Then why do you keep crossing things out?"

One pastor told me of receiving a phone call from a young woman in his congregation. She asked him to reserve a Saturday in the summer for her wedding. Father checked the parish calendar and said the date was open and she could plan the wedding. "When did you become engaged?" he asked.

"Oh, I'm not engaged yet," she answered. "But I have a feeling he's going to ask me on Valentine's Day and I want to be sure we have a good date for the wedding." Such feminine intuition may or may not be correct, but we all engage in similar intuitions at some time or another.

St. Francis of Assisi received a word of direction from God when he was kneeling before the Byzantine cross at San Damiano church in Assisi. "Francis, do you not see that my house is being destroyed? Go and repair it."

Francis presumed that God wanted him to rebuild the crumbling walls of San Damiano. For two years, he lived like a hermit in the wooded area near the church, begging alms and slowly buying stones to repair the dilapidated building. Then the Lord spoke to him again while he was listening to the story of Jesus commissioning the twelve apostles. "As you go preach, say the kingdom of heaven is at hand. Provide neither gold nor silver nor coins in your purses, neither two coats, nor shoes (see Mt. 10:7-10)." Francis knew in his heart that this was a message he was to take to heart. This time the voice of God was confirmed when three other men in the town of Assisi received similar messages from the Bible and went out to the woods to join Francis. Sometimes God gives us a word but it takes time before we can accurately interpret the message.

In order to understand what discernment is, we must first understand what it is not. It is not a form of fortunetelling that gives us data on coming events. A pursuit of fortunetelling accounts for the rising interest in psychics, palm readers, tarot cards, and Ouija boards. People consult tea leaves, the stars and palm readers in an effort to part the curtain that veils the future.

We want to know what the future holds so we will be prepared to face its challenges or so we make the right choices. We don't want to make any mistakes. We often think, if only I had known such and such was going to happen, I could have avoided so much heartache. If we knew in advance all the heartbreak and the disappointments, the unfulfilled dreams and the unrealized hopes, the unconsolable griefs that await us—could we find the courage to venture into the future at all?

Sometimes, it is the mercy of God that does not reveal everything to us. In reality there is no magic prayer, no special novena, no crystal ball, and no favored sign to disclose the future to us. We may not know what the future holds, but we know who holds the future. The goal of discernment is to find God, and in finding him, to know his will. Note the sequence: First we seek him, then his will. For many the sequence is reversed. In true discernment we are meant to discover the wholeness and holiness of God.

True discernment does not wait for the extraordinary but roots itself in our everyday human experiences. It is the recognition of God's voice and call spoken now in the ordinary rather than some esoteric method whispered in our ears during a transcendental moment.

Thus we can understand the wisdom spoken by St. Thérèse of Lisieux, affectionately known as the "Little Flower": "To ecstasy, I prefer the monotony of sacrifice." For little Thérèse, the active reception of the grace that surrounds us, the faithful carrying out of our daily responsibilities, and the willingness to work on our own spiritual growth was truly discerning the will of God.

Thérèse hardly ever had extraordinary prayer experiences, and yet her life was filled with a profound awareness of the presence of Divine Love. She even regarded falling asleep at her prayers as a religious experience. She believed that the monotony of sacrifice, fidelity, and generosity may be the safest and more productive of all religious experience, and it is waiting there for all of us.

This human approach to discernment should not surprise us. Throughout the Scriptures we find God conversing with human beings in language that is understandable, not some indecipherable code that cannot be comprehended. The prophet Jeremiah sums it up beautifully:

> See, the days are coming—it is Yahweh who speaks—when I will make a new covenant with the House of Israel ... deep within them I will plant my Law, writing it on their hearts. Then I will be their God and they will be my people. There will be no further need for neighbor to try to teach neighbor, or brother to say to brother, "Learn to know Yahweh!" No, they will all know me, the least no less than the greatest—it is Yahweh who speaks—since I will forgive their iniquity and never call their sin to mind.
>
> JEREMIAH 31:31, 33-34

This passage points to a basic reality: God's Word reveals truth to us. God has perfectly revealed himself to us in the person of his son, Jesus Christ, "The Word became flesh and dwelt among us" (Jn 1:14).

The Word dwells within each of us to offer guidance, correction, encouragement, and consolation. The true goal of discernment is to learn to know Jesus, and in finding him, to know his will.

Throughout the ages, God has visited his people. Beginning with the Old Testament prophets and continuing to our present-day outpouring of the Holy Spirit, God has always been speaking to us.

For many years, ten-year-old Nick was plagued by irrational fears that gripped him at bedtime. The transition into sleep was repeatedly violated by fear of someone breaking into the house and hurting him. No matter how much his parents reassured him, bedtime was a very troubling experience. One night, when his mother was praying with him, he again said, "Mom, I'm having those scary thoughts. I'm afraid someone will hurt me when I'm sleeping."

Silently the mother prayed, asking God for wisdom. As her son continued to share his apprehension regarding bad people breaking into his house, God clearly gave her the revelation that these thoughts were directly connected to Nick's birth experience. She had never before considered such a correlation.

Nick had nearly bled to death in the womb. During labor, the cord had separated from the placenta, causing severe hemorrhaging, necessitating an emergency C-section and very invasive procedures to save the baby's life. The parents considered his complete recovery and normal development to be a real miracle. But now the Holy Spirit was revealing to Nick's mother what a traumatizing experience it was. His birth was very much like the "breaking and entering" of a robbery. His "safe place" was forcefully violated and a lot of "bad things" were done to save his life.

As God made this known, the mother knew Nick needed inner healing and tried to think of someone who could intercede for him. In the meantime, she decided simply to pray a short prayer asking God to set him free from those old memories. Nick went peacefully to sleep, and from that moment was never again bothered by "bad thoughts" at bedtime.

Discernment was given when the mother asked, listened, and acted on the revelation given to her by the Holy Spirit. She doubted her ability to pray the appropriate prayer, yet the Lord honored her obedience to his Word. God's voice doesn't leave us with feelings of anxiety and fear that are overwhelming. God is love; he does not present us with a message and leave us feeling anxious without pointing out a solution to our anxieties.

An example from Scripture is the message given by God to Ananias saying he must go to Straight Street and lay hands on a man named Saul to give him back his sight. Ananias was very apprehensive but subsequently did as he was directed. God gave Ananias the courage he needed so that the great apostle, Paul, could be set free (see Acts 9:10-19).

The Holy Spirit leaves us confident, not anxious. No matter whether the message is a joyous one or a sobering insight, we feel an inner sense of God's graces. The message might stretch our understanding of our capabilities. Many years ago, when God asked me to put my profession of nursing on the altar and come, follow him, I had no idea where this would lead. I simply took it one step at a time, trusting in the Father's guidance each day.

The voice of God doesn't leave us confused. St. Paul says, "God is a God of order and not confusion (see 1 Cor 14:33)." When I moved to the West Coast in 1988, the prophesies of Nostradamus began making the news. Someone interpreted these ancient writings to predict that the state of California was going to be destroyed by a massive earthquake in May of that year. As my friend

Linda and I drove from Florida along US I-10 in the month of May, we encountered many who were leaving the West Coast, fearing the worst was about to happen. They chided us for being so stubborn in continuing our journey. But each time we prayed, the Holy Spirit seemed to encourage us to keep on going. There were several earthquakes in the ten years I lived in California, but none approached the devastation of those predictions.

God's will does not try to force us into anything. If we feel we have no choice in the matter, then I would question the origin of the message. Free will is our most precious gift from the Creator. Always, we are given a choice to say "yes" or "no." Even the Archangel Gabriel didn't appear to Mary and command, "You are to bear a Son and you must name him Jesus." Mary was given the message and permitted to make her own decision.

All messages from God should make us feel closer to him. Even if the given word convicts us of sin, we still feel loved and affirmed. There is a difference between the conviction of sin given by the Holy Spirit and the condemnation we feel that makes us afraid of God's punishment. When the Spirit speaks to our hearts there is always an opportunity for forgiveness. We can receive the sacrament of reconciliation, do some form of restitution, or tell someone we are sorry for our behavior. In other words, there is a way to atone for the wrongdoing. But when we feel condemned, there is an overwhelming sense of being unacceptable with no recourse to God's mercy.

Whenever such feelings begin to affect our spiritual journey, it's good to reflect on the words of St. Paul: "For I am certain of this: neither death nor life, no angel, no prince, nothing that exists, nothing still to come, not any power, or height or depth, nor any created thing, can ever come between us and the love of God made visible in Christ Jesus our Lord" (Rom 8:38-39).

Any message will become real in God's timing and not ours. Sometimes the Holy Spirit reveals something and we believe it is going to happen "right now." But God's ways are not our ways and God's timing is definitely not ours. For example, Mary, the mother of Jesus, was told, "You are to conceive and bear a son ... He will be great and will be called Son of the Most High. The Lord God will give him the throne of his ancestor David and he will rule over the house of Jacob forever and his reign will have no end (see Lk 1:31-33)." When Mary and Joseph took the infant Jesus to the Temple for the rite of purification, both Anna and Simeon prophesied about the role that Jesus would have in the deliverance of Jerusalem.

Mary may have doubted her ability to hear Gabriel as she watched Jesus working in the carpenter shop and living an ordinary life. He was thirty years old before he began his public ministry. But the Bible tells us in several passages that "Mary treasured all these things and pondered them in her heart" (see Lk 2:19, 51).

She held the vision in her heart until it could be birthed into reality. Mary believed it would come to pass even when she saw no evidence of it. Elizabeth recognized this trait in Mary when she exclaimed, "Yes, blessed is she who believed that the promise made her by the Lord would be fulfilled" (see Lk 1:45).

Discernment requires a willingness to wait upon the Lord's will. Waiting is not considered acceptable in our society. But in God's timing "a thousand years are as a day" (see 2 Pt 3:8).

I wait for Yahweh, my soul waits for him,
I rely on his promise, my soul relies on the Lord
more than a watchman on the coming of dawn
Let Israel rely on Yahweh.

PSALM 130:5-7

Yahweh, my heart has no lofty ambitions,
my eyes do not look too high.
I am not concerned with great affairs
or marvels beyond my scope.
Enough for me to keep my soul tranquil and quiet
like a child in its mother's arms,
as content as a child that has been weaned.

PSALM 131:1-2

It's important to test the spirits giving us messages to be sure they come from God.

It is not every spirit, my dear people,
that you can trust;
test them, to see if they come from God;
You can tell the spirits that come from God by this:
every spirit which acknowledges that Jesus the Christ has come in the flesh is from God;
but any spirit which will not say this of Jesus is not from God,
but is the spirit of Antichrist, whose coming you were warned about ...
Children, you have already overcome these false prophets,
because you are from God and you have in you one who is greater than anyone in this world....

We are children of God, and those who know God
listen to us;
those who are not of God refuse to listen to us.
That is how we can tell the spirit of truth from the
spirit of falsehood.

1 JOHN 4

I once led a pilgrimage to the Holy Land. On the trip
was a man who had exhibited troubled behavior throughout our journey. He was very argumentative with our
guide and kept himself separated from most of the other
pilgrims in our group. One day we took a boat trip across
the Sea of Galilee. As we reached the middle of the lake,
he ran to the railing and tried to jump into the water in
an effort to drown himself. It took several strong men to
subdue him.

Later, he told us the reason for his behavior. The previous night he had read a passage from the Scripture that
he believed was instructing him to take his own life. The
verse he read was an exhortation from St. Paul: "I beg you,
in a way that is worthy of thinking beings, by offering your
living bodies as a holy sacrifice, truly pleasing to God"
(Rom 12:1). He had taken this passage completely out of
context and nearly lost his life because he didn't understand how to perceive the voice of God. The Scriptures
clearly speak the truth of God's desire regarding our lives.

"What I want is love, not sacrifice; knowledge of God, not holocausts" (Hos 6:6).

Prayer for Discernment

Dear Father, I believe you speak to me in many ways. In the beauty of the sunset, in the smile of a child, in the touch of a loved one. But I also believe you speak to my heart, giving me the instructions I need for my earthly journey. Please quicken my ability to hear your voice. Help me to sort out all the opposing messages so I may clearly know your will for my life. Give me sensitive and spiritual ears. Let me know the guidance and direction that will keep me on the right pathway. Help me to trust in your protective arms to safeguard my comings and goings. Thank you for always being there for me. Amen.

Chapter Eight

Confronting Spiritual Warfare

My son, if you aspire to serve the Lord,
prepare yourself for an ordeal.
Be sincere of heart, be steadfast
and do not be alarmed when disaster comes
Cling to him and do not leave him,
so that you may be honored at the end of your days.
Whatever happens to you, accept it,
and in the uncertainties of your humble state,
be patient,
since gold is tested in the fire,
and chosen men in the furnace of humiliation.
Trust him and he will uphold you,
follow a straight path and hope in him.

Sirach 2:1-6

This passage from the ancient book of Sirach is an excellent description of the difficulties Christians can expect to encounter when agreeing to "serve the Lord."

Those who accept a specific task in the Body of Christ, no matter how insignificant the project may appear to be, should "prepare for an ordeal" because all endeavors on behalf of God's kingdom bring us into direct spiritual warfare with the kingdom of darkness. Therefore, it is vitally important that we be prepared to face the turmoil and confusion that often result from serving Jesus Christ.

Christians who have any role of service in prayer meetings frequently experience an unusual number of disturbances leading up to the meeting. Automobiles with flat tires or dead batteries, suddenly-broken household appliances, and misunderstandings among family members are but a few examples of the kind of harassment the enemy sends our way to keep us distracted from the Lord's service.

Dorothy Ranaghan, a long-time leader in the Catholic charismatic renewal, has helped to coordinate numerous spiritual gatherings over the years. She once observed: "Years of experience have convinced me that our hassles will increase almost in direct proportion to the power about to be unleashed at the National Conference of Catholic Charismatics. It would take a huge book to detail for you the stories of sick and even hospitalized children, broken plumbing, flooded basements, during past conferences."[*]

---

[*]Dorothy Ranaghan, "Of Pox and Ants," *New Covenant* (October, 1982): 1.

Anything that disrupts our inner peace is a form of spiritual warfare designed by the enemy to refocus attention away from Jesus Christ and onto the problem at hand. The pattern is nearly always the same: As the time for the prayer meeting, healing service, retreat, or conference draws near, those who have accepted any form of service for the week begin to experience unrest in their spirits.

A certain amount of heaviness and difficulty in praying often referred to as "spiritual travail" begins to descend. Some who are very sensitive to the things of the Spirit become overwhelmed with the need to "pray without ceasing" (see 1 Thes 5:17). Along with this spiritual unrest comes a variety of complications in the home and places of employment. These phenomena affect everyone to some degree—even music and tape ministries, transportation and housing volunteers, and registration personnel. In fact, no one who "aspires to serve the Lord" is immune to some sort of upheaval.

The resulting lack of inner peace can carry over into relationships with family members and fellow Christians, creating tensions in the Body of Christ. It seems that at the time when unity is most important in bringing to birth God's plan, misunderstandings and grievances in the community start to surface. Persons who ordinarily love and respect one another suddenly find themselves bickering over the slightest decision. This is Satan's most subtle and effective weapon—divide and conquer! Once we become alienated and fragmented, the hedge of protection surrounding the group is broken, allowing more confusion and turmoil to erupt.

Such tactics can be avoided if we recognize the truth that "it is not against human enemies that we have to struggle, but against the Sovereignties and the Powers who originate the darkness of this world, the spiritual army of evil in the heavens" (Eph 6:12). The Deceiver tricks us into believing that our enemy is one of our family members or a Christian brother or sister. We become preoccupied with the situation and fail to utilize the spiritual power available to us as believers in Jesus Christ.

In this situation, recognizing the real enemy enables us to employ the proper defense against him. The passage from the book of Sirach gives some very clear advice in this regard: "If you aspire to serve the Lord, prepare yourself for an ordeal" (2:1). Any form of service in the kingdom of God, no matter how humble, will bring some degree of harassment. So it's prudent to prepare for it. Such preparation necessitates a renewed commitment to caring for our spiritual lives.

Prioritizing time for daily private prayer and Scripture

reading is a necessary part of service. Christians in sacramental churches would do well to receive the sacraments of Reconciliation and the Eucharist as frequently as possible. Fasting from any type of self-indulgence grants a greater ability to withstand the temptations of the devil. Many Christians are also discovering the power available through prayerful recitation of the rosary, invoking the intercession of Mary and the saints.

We are encouraged to be "sincere of heart and steadfast" (Sirach 2:2). Differences of opinion may begin to create a strain in relationships with others. But being sincere in expressing our feelings doesn't give us license to wound others. "Even if you are angry, you must not sin; never let the sun set on your anger or else you will give the devil a foothold" (Eph 4:26). God's will can more readily be accomplished through a community united in mind and heart.

"And do not be alarmed when disaster comes" (Sirach 2:2) means that we need not fear the various ways the evil one attempts to distract us from the work we are doing. It helps to develop a sense of humor over distractions and to praise the Lord in the midst of turmoil. The kingdom of darkness dislikes the sounds of joy and praise. Praying in tongues, singing praise-filled songs, and uttering the name of Jesus can be very useful tools in warding off fears and anxieties.

The passage from Sirach also tells us to "be patient, since gold is tested in fire, and chosen men in the furnace of humiliation" (2:5). When we accept a call to serve the Lord, it is God who permits us to go through the subsequent trials in order to purify our motives and burn away all that is not of Him. Those who are truly desirous of following God will not fall by the wayside when trials come, but will persevere in doing His work. On the other hand, those who merely want a glimpse of the glory of the Lord will become easily disenchanted with Christian service when the going gets rough. The dropout rate for the "laborers in the vineyard" is very high!

Spiritual warfare is a normal component of the Christian life. However, we have not been sent into the battle unprepared if we heed the scriptural teachings provided for us. St. Paul's letter to the Ephesians exhorts believers to wear the armor of God: "So stand your ground with truth buckled round your waist, and integrity for a breastplate, wearing for shoes on your feet the eagerness to spread the gospel of peace and always carrying the shield of faith so that you can use it to put out the burning arrows of the evil one. And then you must accept salvation from God to be your helmet and receive the word of God from the Spirit to use as a sword" (Eph 6:14-17).

The first letter of Peter advises: "Be calm and vigilant, because your enemy the devil is prowling round like a roaring lion, looking for someone to eat. Stand up to him, strong in faith and in the knowledge that your brothers all over the world are suffering the same things" (1 Pt 5:8-9).

Our Father has appointed heavenly servants to assist us in our evangelistic endeavors. The book of Revelation tells of the mighty strength given to Michael and his angels in overcoming the attacks of Satan (see Rv 12:7-12). Scripture clearly explains their role in the first chapter of Hebrews: "The truth is they are all spirits whose work is service, sent to help those who will be the heirs of salvation" (Heb 1:14).

I've found this traditional prayer to St. Michael to be invaluable: "St. Michael the Archangel, defend us in the battle; be our protection against the malice and snares of the devil. Rebuke him, O God, we humbly pray, and do thou, O prince of the heavenly host, by the power of God, cast into hell Satan and all the other evil spirits who prowl throughout the world, seeking the ruin of souls. Amen."

In addition, I have come to rely on the use of holy water, blessed salt, and holy oil as effective tools of protection. These elements are infused with powerful blessings to ward off the kingdom of darkness. A woman who had been involved in the occult once told me she experienced a sensation of being touched with flames of fire when someone sprinkled holy water over her before her conversion to Christianity.[*]

If we seriously consider the warnings given in God's Word and prepare for the battle that accompanies service to the Lord, then the warfare will not be a source of division and defeat. Instead, it will become a means of attaining all the Father has planned for us.

Prayer for Protection

"No disaster can overtake you, no plague come near your tent; he will put you in his angel's charge to guard you wherever you go. They will support you on their hands in case you hurt your foot against a stone" (Ps 91:10-12). Father, may the precious blood of Jesus be upon us, upon all our loved ones, upon our homes, upon all those who will be participating in this [gathering, prayer meeting, retreat, conference, etc.]. Protect us from all attacks of the evil one. Send your holy angels to safeguard our mission that it may produce abundant blessings on behalf of your kingdom. Amen

---

[*]For a more detailed explanation of the power of blessed objects, see Francis MacNutt, *Deliverance from Evil Spirits* (Old Tappan, New Jersey: Chosen Books, 1995), chapter 19, "Deliverance Through Blessed Objects," 241–47.

Chapter Nine

$\mathcal{H}$ealing Prayer and Group Meetings

Where two or three meet in my name, I shall be there with them.

Matthew 18:20

Daily private prayer is an important component for the development of a healthy spiritual life. Jesus said, "when you pray, go to your private room and, when you have shut your door, pray to your Father who is in that secret place, and your Father who sees all that is done in secret will reward you" (Mt 6:6). The Scriptures tell us of several occasions when Jesus sent the crowds away and went off by himself to pray.

However, he also taught the importance of collective prayer when he said, "If two of you on earth agree to ask anything at all, it will be granted to you by my Father in heaven. For where two or three meet in my name, I shall be there with them" (Mt 18:19-20). Somehow the effectiveness of prayer is heightened with the additional agreement of others. This may help to explain the recent proliferation of worldwide intercessory prayer groups.

I frequently receive letters from others relating how they interceded for a particular need but saw little progress until they submitted the petition for group prayer. One woman was greatly surprised when her dad began attending church services. For many years he had refused to accompany the family to Sunday Mass, and she had nearly stopped praying for his conversion. One night she attended a local prayer gathering and asked the members to remember her dad. The next Sunday he joined the rest of the family and has continued to do so.

Sometimes the "death to self" involved in admitting our needs to others is a factor in opening the door. Most often it is the power offered by the body of believers that makes the difference. When we gather to praise and worship the Lord, there seems to be a tangible current of divine energy flowing through the group. Often a prayer room seems to become warmer as prayer is offered and people begin removing coats and sweaters.

This current of love provides a sense of closeness to God and to one another. It becomes easier to believe in the Father's care and concern for his creation. This is often reflected in the loving attitude of brothers and sisters who join us in prayer. It is much easier to believe God is interested in answering our needs when we sense the empathic feelings around us.

We can contribute to this spiritually beneficial climate by our thoughtful consideration of others. One way is by becoming attentive through nonjudgmental loving and listening. Such undivided attention and interest can also foster a deeper attitude of compassion and understanding. The word "compassion" literally means to "feel with another." It requires the listener to hear the other's words in order to comprehend his or her position. Only if we have bothered to walk for a while in another's shoes can we possibly begin to realize the extent of his or her feelings. Then, like St. Paul, we may "rejoice with those who rejoice and be sad with those in sorrow" (Rom 12:15).

Learning to be nonjudgmental in listening requires a bit of practice since most of us have a tendency to be suspicious of viewpoints opposing our own. It can be a sign of maturity to accept others as they are, thereby realizing the wisdom of Paul's observation, "you together are Christ's body; but each of you is a different part of it" (1 Cor 12:27).

My experience with prayer groups has convinced me that everyone has a deep-seated need to be heard, affirmed, and accepted. Even those who appear to possess great ego-strength bloom more openly in the powerful environment of loving, caring people. Jesus, with all his sensitivity, must have been aware of the faults of his disciples, yet he chose to concentrate on their attributes, enabling them to do great things.

Most of us are so overtly conscious of our failings at perfection that we really need others to point out our good qualities to us. Of course, there are situations when people may need to be confronted about certain attitudes or actions that are destructive to themselves or others. Yet even this can be accomplished through the gift of love. The teaching of St. Augustine to despise the sin yet love the sinner is a goal worth attaining.

A significant number of people initially become involved in prayer groups due to a crisis situation that prompts them to seek spiritual help. Therefore, most prayer gatherings devote a portion of their meetings to praying for the needs of others. When a group is small enough it is not uncommon for everyone to participate in praying over individuals for specific intercessions, but this becomes unrealistic in large assemblies. As a solution to this problem, many groups designate prayer teams to minister on a personal basis.

These teams can consist of two or more persons who have sensitive hearts and a deep desire to bring the healing love of Jesus to others. The best criteria for discerning whether or not someone is a healthy instrument of intercessory prayer can take the form of questions regarding the outcome of the prayer.

Does the person being prayed for feel closer to God after the prayer than before?

The prayed-for individual may still seem physically unhealed, but does he or she sense the Father's merciful love and tender care?

Can he or she trust the answer will be forthcoming in God's timing?

The following prayer can be a powerful weapon against the forces of darkness. It is a prayer of protection recommended for each prayer team prior to their time of ministry.

Prayer Before Ministering

In the name of Jesus Christ, and by the power of his cross and blood, I bind up any evil spirits, forces and powers of earth, air, fire or water, of the nether world and the satanic forces of nature. By the sword of the Spirit and in the authority given to me by Jesus Christ, I break any curses, hexes, or spells and send them back to where they came from. I plead the protection of the shed Blood of Jesus Christ on [our meeting, my family, the church, my ministry, etc.] and command that any

departing spirits leave quietly, without causing distur-
bance, and go straight to Jesus Christ for him to deal
with them as he sees fit.

I bind any demonic interaction, interplay, or commu-
nications. I claim the protection of the shed Blood of
Jesus Christ over [name it—this place, a person, etc.].
Amen.

The following are suggestions that may help to
increase the effectiveness of prayer teams.

1) *The prayer room should be reasonably quiet and comfortable
   with a meditative atmosphere.* Distractions make it difficult to concentrate on prayer. Therefore, the place
   for refreshments and fellowship ought to be removed
   from the area designated for ministry.

2) *If possible, the prayer room should be available before the gen-
   eral group meeting as well as afterwards.* Many times
   people attend the prayer session for the sole purpose
   of receiving personal ministry and are, sometimes,
   too burdened or ill to sit through an entire meeting.
   Providing an opportunity for people to obtain prayer
   before the meeting can also help to reduce the number of prayer requests at the end of the meeting.

3) *Before beginning to minister, the team should pray over one another for the fullness of the Holy Spirit's gifts to flow through each of them.* Team members may occasionally require prayer for a problem in their own lives before reaching out to others. It is also difficult to be an instrument for the healing love of Jesus when harboring feelings of resentment or anger. Here is a prayer that can be used for this purpose.

Prayer That God Will Use Us

Dear Jesus, help me to spread your fragrance
everywhere I go.
Flood my soul with your Spirit and life.
Penetrate and possess my whole being so utterly,
that my life may only be a radiance of you.
Shine through me and be so in me
that every soul I come in contact with
may feel your presence in my spirit.
Let them look up and see no longer me
but only Jesus!

Stay with me
and then I shall begin to shine as you shine,
as to be a light for others.
The light of Jesus will be all from you.
It will be you shining on others through me.

Let me thus praise you without preaching by words,
but by my example,
by the catching force of the sympathetic influence
of what I do, the evident fullness of the love
my heart bears to you. Amen.

John Henry Cardinal Newman

4) *Whenever possible, people should be prayed over individually rather than in groups.* This gives the team an opportunity to concentrate on the specific prayer request of the person. Jesus asked blind Bartimaeus, "What do you want me to do for you?" (Mk 10:51). It was surely obvious to the Lord that this man was blind, but Jesus wanted him to specify the need. Many prayers go unanswered because we fail to identify what we want.

---

*John Henry Newman, Selected Sermons, Prayers and Devotions, ed. John Thorton and Susan Varenne (New York: Vintage, 1999), 340–1.

5) *Protect the person being prayed over from the confusion of too many discernments, prophecies, or words of knowledge from the prayer team.* It's best to assign one person to lead the prayer while the other team members support the prayer.

6) *The prayer team should never direct an individual to discontinue medication, treatment, or therapy.* The healing love of Jesus also operates through the physician's expertise. If an inspiration truly comes from the Spirit, it will be confirmed through the natural order.

7) *The prayer team should develop a sense of unity with one another that allows the gifts of the Holy Spirit to flow through the entire praying body so no one person dominates every situation.* The body of Christ functions most effectively when all its parts are operating.

8) *After ministry has been completed, it's important for the team to pray a cleansing prayer for one another.* The following is an example of such a prayer.

Prayer After Ministering

Lord, Jesus Christ, thank you for sharing with us your wonderful ministry of healing and deliverance. Please cleanse us of any sadness, negativity, or sickness that we may have picked up while interceding for others. If evil spirits attached themselves to oppress or control any of us, we command you, spirits of earth, air, fire, or water, of the nether world or of nature, to depart now and go straight to Jesus for him to deal with as he will. Come, Holy Spirit, renew us and fill us anew with your power, love, and joy. Wherever we feel weak or drained of energy, strengthen us with your power and light. Fill us with renewed life. Send your holy angels to minister to all our family members. Guard and protect them and us from all sickness or accidents. We ask these things in Jesus' holy name. Amen.

Praying for the needs of others can be a fulfilling and rewarding ministry even for those who are not yet healed themselves. The unselfishness involved in reaching out a helping hand can open up the door for great blessings. One research study involved taking samples of blood from persons before and after they received prayer. Laboratory tests showed the immune system to be healthier after prayer. The same tests were performed on the ministering individuals, demonstrating similar results. Praying for others seems to bring an overflow of graces into our own lives and areas of need. It's interesting to note how many recognized miracles occurred at Lourdes, France, while a person was praying for someone else to be cured.

I have many beloved friends who are themselves disabled, yet they never hesitate to bring the healing love of Jesus to those in need. Some are blind, in wheelchairs, or paralyzed, but God works through them in powerful ways.

Consecration to the Ministry of Healing

Father, God of all creation, I believe you called me to serve you as I minister to those who suffer in mind, body, or spirit. I offer myself today in fuller consecration of my life, my work and my profession to the vocation of healing into which God calls me. I sincerely desire to seek mental, physical, and spiritual health for myself and actively to nurture whatever gifts or talents have been granted to me by the Holy Spirit. I endeavor to share God's compassionate love with others through my personal stories, my prayers, and my works of mercy. I offer my hands and my heart to those who desire wholeness in body, mind and spirit. Amen.